When Robert Burns Came to Tea & Other Poems

Bridget Nolan

When Robert Burns came to Tea and Other Poems

Published by The Conrad Press in the United Kingdom 2022

Tel: +44(0)1227 472 874
www.theconradpress.com
info@theconradpress.com

ISBN 978-1-915494-28-3

Copyright © Bridget Nolan, 2022

All rights reserved. Typesetting and Cover Design by:
Charlotte Mouncey, www.bookstyle.co.uk

The Conrad Press logo was designed by Maria Priestley.

Printed and bound in Great Britain by Clays Ltd, St Ives plc

For my husband, Frank

Author's note

I spent some time thinking about how I wanted the titles of my poems to read. In my first anthology, I chose to use capital letters on each of the key words and I was happy with that. I do like to play around with structure though and I wanted to try something different in this second collection. I tried using a capital letter only at the very beginning of each title but it didn't look right; to me, the words looked like unconnected sentences on their own. The lines looked out of place.

So I decided to use a capital letter on the first word of each poem's title, along with a capital on the last word. It works for me.

Contents

Author's note..4

When Robert Burns came to Tea..7
The ladder in my Tights..9
We're on the same Road..11
The river from Rochester Pier..12
In the woods with Mum and Dad....................................13
When we were Young...14
The ghost of a life lived: Violet..15
Higher and Wider..16
Higher and Wider II...18
The tears won't Stop..19
The world and Beyond..20
Wonderwall..21
The drunk and the Druggie..22
The candle in the Library...23
Old People..24
Inferior...26
Five pairs of eyes looking at my Thing..............................28
On my own in the Café..30
Moon II..31
Niamh's Song...32
Why would I Imagine?...34
Boxley Beginnings..35
New Year's Day with You..36
There are no Fairies...37
In the sea at Hythe...38
Beard Logic..39
A Dickens 2020..40
The exasperation of Mrs Dickens.....................................42
St Francis School Days...44
The Saturday pictures Gang...45

Mouse's Revenge	46
40 and Judging	47
Exclusivity	48
Liar	49
Suffolk Breakers	50
Us Girls	51
A thought for Time	52
The man in the Suit	53
Thief	54
Buttercups	55
Us two and you Two	56
A new Morning	57
Snow	58
Father Christmas has a bad Day	59
JCC	61
Being 50	62
On a steam train on the Watercress Line	64
Social Denial	65
Tiny Steps	66
Rain on Me	67
Feel	67
Umbrella	68
The pain splits me in Two	69
Child of Change	70
The Rooks	71
Bob Ross	72
Yesterdays	73
Come love me, Autumn	74
Christmas Years	75
Early morning home Town	77
Notes to Poems	79
About the Author	94
Acknowledgements	96

When Robert Burns came to Tea

Oh, Robert Burns. Well, Rab, to me.
I asked him round my house to tea.
The table creaked beneath the spread
Of cakes and cheese and pies and bread
And sweets and treats and pasta bake.
I even made a haggis cake.

We chatted. It was going fine.
He drank the scotch, I stuck to wine
But then, perplexed, he stopped mid-word
And asked, 'what is that noise I heard?'
'It's just my little mice,' I said,
'There's Gordon, Alistair and Jed.'

Well, as I introduced my meeces
To my shock, Rab went to pieces;
Became a terrified, tim'rous beastie,
Quite put the mockers on our feastie.
'Come Rab,' you must buck up,' I said,
'I'll put them outside, in the shed.'

My meeces gone, we chatted more
But, oh, he turned out such a bore.
He told me all about his love;
'She must be sent from heav'n above,
Wondrous as a red, red rose.'
Do you know, he got right up my nose.

Kept banging on about this stuff,
By nine o'clock, I'd had enough.
I hinted it was time to go.
Sing Auld Lang Syne? I don't think so!
Oh, how I wanted him to leave;
His smugness had begun to cleave.

All his clever, witty banter;
Stories about Tam O'Shanter.
I told him it was getting late
And waved him off from my front gate.
'I'll come again,' he called with glee.
He won't, not if it's down to me.

Oh no mate, not on your nelly.
Next time, I'll be inviting Shelley.

The ladder in my Tights

I had a hunch it was going to be one of those nights
And the last thing I needed was a ladder in my tights.
I'd left my glasses in the office so I didn't see
The cat along the hallway and I spun A over T.

I'd been dreaming of the company, the food and the sex
When I started off my weekend with a bang and hit the decks.
So, visually challenged with a buzzing in my head,
I made my way upstairs and slowly sat upon the bed.

I took a few deep breaths then washed and changed my gear;
I couldn't tell if things were far away or, more like... here.
Then I spilt nail varnish on my favourite skirt
And I smeared some red lipstick on the collar of my shirt.

I could just sense I looked like one of life's less pretty sights
So I changed into a dress with my sheer expensive tights.
With great care, I rolled them and slipped the legs over my feet.
Softly, I placed them on the floor and got up from my seat.

Then I heard my phone alarm; I was running out of time.
He'd be waiting there for me with my vodka, slice and lime
And I pulled upon my tights with such great ferocity
That my nails skimmed along them with immense velocity.

My stress level moved to the most impressive dizzy heights
When I could feel the vast, stupendous ladder in my tights.
So I hid the sorry mess under a long skirt and boots
And later, in the restaurant, I coloured to my roots

When I sat down at the wrong table and kissed the wrong face
And the dishes on the menu danced all over the place.
After eating, I discovered I'd forgotten my purse;
It was on the kitchen side with my door keys which was worse.

He smiled and looked at me with awful pity in his eyes;
We agreed, my treat next time, before saying our goodbyes.
I just knew that it was going to be one of those nights
And the least of my worries was the ladder in my tights.

We're on the same Road

Young eyes look at me, pity circling around the irises
Before the pupils narrow in contempt.
I hold my ground, shifting from one creaky knee to the other
And leaning in slightly with my good ear.
'You need to open those eyes,' I say,
'You need to open those eyes and look around you.
Look down at your feet and mine.
You will see that we are both walking the same stony road.
I'm just a little bit further along it, that's all.'

The river from Rochester Pier

I watch from the pier
As the hard, tightly rolled ripples scrape over the compacted mud;
They look dirty
And they look beautiful.
The hum of the busy traffic on the bridge
Dulls their sound to my ears but still I hear them,
In my mind.
Further out, the swirling eddies twist and rush
Like miniature liquid cyclones,
Sucking in the detritus floating on the water.
The prison hulks were here once upon a lifetime;
Just there, where the plush motor boats
Bob around along the jetty.
Underneath, in the dark wealthy shadows,
Lie someone's pennies, someone's file, someone's gun;
Maybe a trinket shaped from bone or a whistle
Hewn by the hands of some wretched soul.

To the right, the tidal water shimmies along
Towards Chatham docks,
Less thriving now but busy and still breathing.
Out, out, out to the Red Sand Towers and beyond.
Sometimes I see a lone seal, rolling around in the peace of the present.
And there, to the left, the afternoon sunshine
Caresses the whole width of the river
As it glides towards me from Allington Lock.
Many eyes have watched this same body of water
And many more will follow it out to sea.
The Medway, my old friend;
Out you go, with a little bit of me.
Tomorrow I shall be here again
And you can put me back together.

In the woods with Mum and Dad

When I was young, I feared the woods;
Dark and eerie, creeping with crawlies,
Crackling with footsteps and sneaking with eyes.
You made me feel brave with a word and a wave.

We soaked up the sun through the trees;
We marvelled at the birds and the squirrels
Or stood still and watched as a fox tripped by.
I remember that sometimes I felt so happy.

Today, when we went to the woods,
We held hands as we picked our way
Over icy bracken and muddy paths.
I noticed things are different somehow.

We had to step so carefully;
The leaves were wet; the puddles were deep
And I was afraid for different reasons.
I could see that we are all children now.

When we were Young

When we were young
You loved me.
What else was there to love?

Watching telly with home-cooked grub;
Late nights with your mates in the local pub;
Clean clothes and a cosy warm bed;
Worry-free with space in your head.

There are other things now
For you to love
And only my love gives them meaning.

The ghost of a life lived: Violet

This yard harbours the ghost of a life lived,
Gliding softly through the salty mist
And peeping in the glassless portholes on the boat.
The whispers creep along the ground
And tremble up the tree trunks,
Clinging to the ivy leaves like ageless honey.
The rusted blade on the forgotten saw bench
Smiles a hideous smile at nobody.
This yard evinces a palpable spirit;
An invisible, naked, restless spirit
That walks among the weeds and silt,
Looking for a place to sleep.
The water slaps the hull and bleeds
Across the pockmarks on the metal.
A television aerial snaps about on top of a pole;
A severed washing line twirls around on the ground
Like an angry snake, its tail still tied through a ring on a tree.

This yard is sad and neglected.
A life lived; but whose?
Hardened cement, the bag disintegrating,
Dumped upon a plant pot that has cracked with the strain.
The weight of time bears down on this yard
And I wonder when it will be noticed;
When it will be revived and used again.
I try to imagine how the ghost might feel
When the living move back in,
Sweeping away the dusty, tired out
Remnants of a past life lived.
This yard could be my life
And I like to think the spirit can let go,
Allowing the here and now to
Breathe this place into a new existence.

Higher and Wider

There are too many of us including the pets;
Dad's threatened them all again with the vets.
If we all breathe in, we must all breathe out
And there's definitely no room to shake it all about.

There's a serious case of congestion upstairs
And below is a worrying state of affairs.
There are too many coats hanging on the hooks
And the bookshelf's creaking under all our books.
If we all breathe in, we must all breathe out
And there's really no room to shake it all about.

Is that wet gloss on the dog's backside?
We'll leave it and pick it off when it's dried.
Put that down and don't do that,
You know there's no room to swing the cat.
Tell your sister I've found her red welly;
It's by the ironing board, next to the telly.
If we all breathe in, we must all breathe out
And there's simply no room to shake it all about.

Remember, we must form an orderly queue
If more than one of us requires the loo.
Take it in turns to squeeze round the table;
I swear, it'd give us more room in a stable.

If we all be patient and try to be nice,
We could model ourselves on a family of mice;
Looking out for each other and snuggling up
In our family home where we all get to sup
On the Sunday wine, cheap and cool,
Mopped up with bread from our genetic pool.
So if we all breathe in, we must all breathe out.
No matter if we cannot shake it all about
For if we all breathe in and we all breathe out,
We know we're alive.

Higher and Wider II

We all breathed in and we all breathed out;
We all breathed in and they all moved out;
We both breathed in and we both breathed out
And there is copious room to shake it all about.

But we don't like it; the space is cold;
The space is empty and we feel old.
We want to be tired, squashed and stressed.
They all moved out and who'd have guessed
The echoes make our eardrums ache;
The whispers make our senses quake;
The shadows make our heart rates rise;
The chasm swallows up our cries.

We both breathed in and we both breathed out
But we can't even hear each other shout.
Slowly the silence suffocates us
And so, we think, without any fuss
We'll lie down now and die.

The tears won't Stop

Determined to laugh my way through life,
The energy is squeezed out of me
As I keep my deep emotions hid
In my fragile glass heart with the tightly shut lid.

I tip from one day into the next,
Pouring myself into this person
I'm supposed to be. But it's not me;
My spirit is trapped and I want to be free.

And people; I don't think they suspect
What a heavy load I drag around.
They wouldn't understand the matter;
They don't know how easily my heart may shatter

If those emotions begin to stir,
Triggered by a sight, a word or a song.
The pressure will force the lid to blow
And I will collapse, distraught and the tears will flow.

If they should break out from their vessel,
The tears will flow and the tears won't stop.
Nobody knows how much my arms ache.
Nobody knows, but one trip and my heart will break.

The world and Beyond

How much do I love you? As big as the world and beyond.
You talk to me, all serious and grown up,
Enjoying your possession of a five-year-old's wisdom;
Explaining to me something you watched on the television
And what your teacher told you about Jesus.
I am all ears and awe.

My dewey eyes reflect in yours, all sparkling in pure love.
You laugh as you jump on my knee and I squeeze you tight to
my body.
How is it that someone so tiny
Can make me, so old, feel this way?

I thought I had used up my youthful sense of wonder;
I felt weary and scared of the future.
Then I was given you, my darling, and these days belong to us.
I must learn all I can from you
As we tread this unknown path together.
You bring me fun and laughter, worry and hope
And I love you as big as the world and beyond.

Wonderwall

'Again,' she says, 'again.'
So I put on the CD and she dances;
She wiggles her little bum
And her little knees bend.
There's no co-ordination but she knows that's what we do when we dance.
She changes her tempo and sways from side to side
Then her tiny shoes tap on the kitchen floor tiles
As she performs a little shuffle.
She decides to twirl around which isn't easy
When she's clutching her two baby dollies
And she stumbles but recovers and goes straight into another bum wiggle.
All the time, she is listening for the end of the song,
Ready to say, 'again, again.'
I'm laughing and smiling;
Sometimes I sing along and always, I can't take my eyes off her.
She is my little wonderwall.

The drunk and the Druggie

The drunk and the druggie live on the hill;
One craves a drink and the other needs a pill.
They live in a house constructed of cards
And the path from the road is made of glass shards.
This leads to the front door, cheerless and bare
And the doorbell rings out a dull, loveless air.
The drunk sits alone sipping vino and beer;
If his heart wasn't dead, he might shed a tear.
But his heart *is* dead; he has nothing to give;
An emotionless husk that knows not how to live.
The druggie sits in a room on her own,
Holding on to her spleen like a dog with a bone.
She despises him for his weakness and sloth
So she takes another pill as she mutters an oath.

To break the impasse, he buys her a gift;
She laughs at him and widens the rift.
He retreats to his room and downs a few beers
And keeps himself hidden away from his peers
For fear his dissembling existence is shown
And his miserable life on the hill becomes known.
She taunts him and mocks him and makes him feel small
As she grins at his face through her dark dusty pall.

Turns out that materials can't fill the holes
In their lives, in their hearts, in the depths of their souls.
The drunk and the druggie live on the hill.
One craves a drink and the other needs a pill.

The candle in the Library

As I look in my mind's mirror, I notice that I look like an owl;
Dark rings around my eyes and crows' feet. Owls' feet.
The dull, dusty purple candle reflecting my psyche
With its deathly blackened wick.
I can feel only death and destruction as I hold it,
Cold and hard in my tired arthritic fingers.
I want to throw it but people around the table are looking at me so I smile
And I write my piece of prose:
She used the warm wax to stick the candle onto a pink saucer.
Always pink. Always pink.
My cloak begins to tighten around my neck and I'm growing hot
When the bright, encouraging sound of a voice in control
Helps me back into the here and now
And I light the candle with a taper of hope
As I turn my prose into a poem.

Old People

As I sit by the window, I watch them.
She takes his hand before stepping into the road then slowly,
So worryingly slowly, they reach the other side.
She keeps hold of his hand as they ascend towards the pub door,
Placing each foot carefully upon each step.
'Morning,' the waitress calls cheerfully, 'your table's ready.'
The old lady helps him take off his jacket
Then takes hold of his hand again as he carefully sits down.
'Just our usual, dear,' she says to the young woman
And the waitress doesn't need to write anything down on her little notepad.
Returning with a pint of beer and a cup of tea,
She places them in front of the old lady
Who looks at her man with a smile.
Gently, she places his hands around the glass and steadies it
As he lifts it to his lips then slowly, slowly, they eat their meal,
The old lady cutting up his food for him.
Not a word passes between them.
As I watch, I feel myself pulled into their silent world
And the chatter around us melts into nothingness.

Just for a while I share their existence in this world
Though they don't see me here.
The old man has finished eating and his lady tenderly wipes his mouth with a napkin.
He smiles as she lifts his pint to his lips and her eyes twinkle.
The waitress returns to clear the table and the old lady takes out her purse
Before paying the special senior citizens' rate
Then the two women help him put on his jacket.
I gaze as they leave, his hand held tightly in hers.
They descend the steps, cross the road and disappear into the rest of their lives
Just as mine forces itself upon me, the surrounding noises crushing my senses.
I feel the heat as a tear gently ploughs a furrow down my cheek.

Inferior

I'm not sure I wanted to come here today
And it's an awful lot of money to pay;
Just look at the cost of an afternoon tea.
You get their attention. I must have a pee...

That's better.
But look at that man over there;
He's fixed on me with an imperious stare.
I suppose he thinks that I'm not good enough
To sit here surrounded by all this posh stuff.
I tell you, I don't like his manner at all;
With that attitude, he's got some gall.

Have you ordered?
Well, I'll just get us a drink;
I need to wind down or I'll kick up a stink.

There you are...
He's still at it; look at his face
As he looks down his nose like he owns the place.
He's really beginning to get on my goat;
He looks like he's making a mental note
Of the clothes I'm in and the brand of my shoes
And he's probably radioed someone who'll
Arrive with a team of security men.
They'll escort me and eject me outside just when
Some opportunist journalist snaps my mug
And they'll make me out to be some kind of thug!

Look, he's coming over.
I told you; you'll see...

Look mate, you've clearly got a problem with me.
You've made me uneasy; you've spoilt my time here.
You don't think I fit in; you've made that quite clear.
I want to know your name. I'll contact your boss.
I won't come here again; oh yes, it's your loss.
You look at me like I'm only good for cleaning floors –

Madam!
What?

I only meant to say... ahem... your skirt is tucked inside your drawers.

Five pairs of eyes looking at my Thing

The silence chews at my bones
As I walk towards the chair.
They all smile kindly as my embarrassment suffocates the air.

'Make yourself at home,' says Nurse.
Home? Is she in the same room?
I'm in a freak show and the star of this show is my flamin' womb!

'Wiggle down a bit, dear,'
Says the pleasant professor
As he gets comfy; I try to imagine he's my hairdresser.

I focus on the ceiling
As they fiddle with my bits
And keep my mind on The Bee Gees while I recall their greatest hits.

'I'm going in,' says the prof
As he twangs his rubber glove.
I think *Jive Talking* and swiftly move on to *How Deep is Your Love?*

As I remember *Night Fever*
I feel a real urge to sing
But it soon subsides as five pairs of eyes start looking at my thing.

The young junior doctor
Throws me a big cheesy grin.
He's keen to impress so picks up some gadget and gets stuck in.

I'm alone with Barry Gibb
And he lets me stroke his beard
'More Than a Woman,' he whispers and it doesn't feel at all weird.

'All finished,' says the main man
So I let the Bee Gees go
But as I'm leaving, I feel uneasy and somehow I just know

That now, when I hear their tunes
My eyes are going to sting
Because all I'll see is five pairs of eyes looking at my thing.

On my own in the Café

I thought I'd be ok with this; I've done it before
But I'm not sure today as I walk through the door
And a couple of heads turn to look at me.

Too late, I've made my decision; I'm seeing it through.
I take a seat, careful not to engage with those who
Feel they should offer me a pitying look.

I left my confidence behind or lost it somewhere.
I check my pockets and look in my bag; not there.
So today I use my emergency smile.

I lift it from my memory and stick it in place
So no-one can tell when they scrutinize my face
How my tinnitus screams and my blood flows fast.

I order myself a cream tea then take out my pad
And my pen… nothing… and today I wish I had
A friend to sit across the table from me.

I'm too tired to be alone in this cosy crowd.
I jot down a few words as I keep my head bowed
Then I pour out the tea and split the fresh scone.

The idle chit chat warms me up and my mind takes flight;
The words flow and, with them, the world starts to look bright
As I hover above my life down below.

The café owner smiles at me as I go to pay.
Outside, I'm swallowed up by the relentless day,
Ingested by life. And I'm all right with that.

Moon II

Here I am, talking to you again.
How can I not,
When you draw me outside on this squally cold night?
My path is lit by a chattering of stars,
Scattered across the sky with the flick of an invisible hand.
I'm entranced by your kind face,
The warm beam of the out of sight sun highlighting your craggy features,
Past the skeletal trees that stretch across your orb,
All those miles away.
The tiniest drops of water drizzle down on my face
As if that same invisible hand has shaken a cloud,
Releasing sweet hundreds and thousands.
It tastes good, this night.
I stare at your brilliance, hard and long until I feel my eyes hurt.
All around me, the plants and the hedges,
The trees and the creatures, the stars and the clouds
Disappear and we two are all that exists.
A darkness sweeps across my vision as the rain falls with more serious intent
And I must go indoors.
So, gently, I tuck you up inside my mind
And carry you upstairs to bed.

Niamh's Song

I'm here with you for all time;
It's our time, don't doubt it.
My heart's there in your heart;
You're never without it.

Hello stars, hello sky, hello tree.
Look at me;
Feel the warmth of my love,
Feel my soul as it watches the sea.

Hello clouds, hello breeze, hello moon.
Look at me;
See the smile in my eyes
As our mother Earth plays me a tune.

I'm here with you for all time;
It's our time, don't doubt it.
My heart's there in your heart;
You're never without it.

Hello sun, hello rain, hello snow.
Look at me;
Hear the joy in my laugh
As I'm watching the sweet rivers flow.

Hello you, all those people I love.
Look at me;
Feel my breath on your face
As I fly by your side like a dove.

I'm here with you for all time;
It's our time, don't doubt it.
My heart's there in your heart;
You're never without it.

I'm here with you for all time;
It's our time, don't doubt it.
My heart's there in your heart;
You're never without it.

Why would I Imagine?

Why would I try and imagine what you may have been like now?
Why would I see your gappy smile beaming back at me?
Why would I try and guess if the colour of your hair changed?
Or feel it in my hands as I gently tie ribbons in your plaits?

How could I picture the image of you as you put your dolly in her pram?
And how would I know your favourite story book?
How could I know your best friend's name?
And why would I hear you sing me a nursery rhyme?

There is no time for heartbreaking 'I wonders.'
You showed me the miracle of life.
Why would I try and imagine what you may have been like now
When you live here in my heart?

I met you. And that must be enough.

Boxley Beginnings

Here I stand, in Boxley Village, where it all began;
I was just a girl and he my teenage man.
The old cobbled floor and the big Belfast sink;
We had no inclination to ever stop and think
But moved in with our auction house treasure
And lived seven years through our trials and our pleasure.
Three babies grew under the countryside sky
With our dog and our cats and our rabbits and I
Can picture them right now, running around
In the field by the Church and they laughed when they found
Big shiny conkers in the long damp grass.
Uninterested sheep grazed as we all walked past
And the big old cows allowed us to share their space
But I remember how we all quickened our pace
As we walked along the edge of the horses' enclosure,
Feeling anxious not to disturb their composure.
On the lane, we waited for the bang of the cherry orchard gun
And watched the birds take flight in the Autumnal sun.

New Year's Day with You

We both felt the sadness emanating from the walls
And creeping in underneath the doors;
So we did what we always do
And went to Hythe.

I recall it was around midday when we arrived.
We parked up the car, put on our coats
And walked towards some peace of mind
By the seaside.

I took your hand and we fell in close against the wind.
As we ventured towards old Folkestone,
We felt ourselves swallowed up by
The rolling sea.

Before we reached Sandgate, we crossed the road to walk back
Beside our old friend, the canal.
The loud silence thrilled and spooked us;
Just you... and me.

We practically ran up the path by the golf course,
Across the road and back into
The grip of the fresh salt spray,
Towards Dymchurch.

The chilly air caught the back of our throats and we laughed
As the wind propelled us along.
The sadness settled down to sleep
And we lived on.

There are no Fairies

Holding hands, we strolled around the garden,
Looking for signs of the resident fox.
Disturbing a mouse, we begged its pardon
As we rummaged around in a pile of old rocks.

'Look,' he cried, 'there's my big dinosaur bones!'
They were hidden where he left them last time,
Underneath his stash of last year's pine cones,
Covered with busy insects and shiny slug slime.

We wandered over to our magic tree;
I asked, 'is that a tuft of monster hair?'
'I think so,' he said, 'but it won't get me
And anyway, it might just be a bear.'

I was the person waiting for the train
At the station, by the green water tank
And he got to be the driver again,
Buffering up to our favourite plank.

'Shh, look,' I whispered, 'the fairies are there,
Behind that moss-covered bicycle wheel.'
He fixed me with an incredulous stare;
'Nanny, there *are* no fairies; they're *not real.*'

So we held hands as we sauntered indoors,
Through the bird song and the hum of the bee.
Inside, we heard the low dinosaur roars;
We ignored it and settled down to our tea.

In the sea at Hythe

Come on in;
I'd like to say the water's warm but it isn't.
In fact, it's freezing and I'm not laughing.
I'm coughing and wheezing.

The sun's out;
It glistens on the rippled waves and it dazzles,
Making me squint. There's nothing like it;
Soft as oil; hard as flint.

As I swim,
I feel the sand-yellow water envelope me.
It sticks to my hair; I lay on my back
And my soul drinks the air.

The salt heals
As it dries out my cares and my fears; I can feel it
Running in my veins, falling from my eyes
And washing off the stains

From a mind
Much troubled by a fretful world. A seagull calls
As it skims the sea. I stay on my back
And the water drowns me.

It feels good.
It feels heavy on my stomach. My eyes are shut;
I can see faces and hands that beckon,
Calling me to places

I should know.
I relax and give myself up but I'm alone.
I become aware that the salt stings my eyes,
And I can smell life in the air.

So I'm here,
Stretched out on the pebbles of hope, coated in foam
Whipped up by the now and the way back when,
A little more sure of the why and the how.

Beard Logic

I think Granddad should grow a beard.
Why don't you ask your Daddy to grow a beard?
Don't be silly, my Daddy's got hair!

A Dickens 2020

What right do you have, Mr Dickens, to thrust upon the world
Your morbid observations of the worst of humankind
And your ridiculous interpretation of the myriad character
traits of our sorry race?

Did you assume it would entertain us?
Did you think you had the power to move us?
Did you imagine you would compel us to look inside our own
hearts
For compassion? For conscience? For what?
What business is it of ours, the life of Jo the road sweeper?
How can we change the fate of Little Nell
Or stop old Havisham's abuse of young Pip?

But here's the squeeze; here's the cause for unease
As we reflect upon your death 150 years ago
From our vantage point here in 2020, the beginning of our
Covid era.

So Nell's grandfather's gambling habit leads to her death
As the ads on the telly invite us to change our lives; to become
a winner.
Richard Carstone wastes his time in pursuit of what's rightfully
his,
Puppet and plaything of the judicial system that ties him up in
adjournment
And red tape, slowly strangling the young man until he dies.
While we abuse the same system in the desire for
compensation,

Our victimhood culture refusing to accept that stuff happens in life.
We must pick ourselves up and struggle on
Until we receive that fateful call, offering help
With regard to that accident we recently had.

Oh, I imagine you think yourself clever, don't you Mr Dickens?
Or were you simply wise enough to know
That human behaviour goes round and round and on and on.

Nothing really changes.
Take those Cratchits; so poor they'd qualify for benefits today
And free school dinners; little children, thin and hungry.
And here we sit, stuffed and dozy, fingering our keypads and watching the ads;
Another takeaway, another bet, another purchase as our shops go down the sink.

I concede, Mr Dickens, you have made us think.
There is a glimmer of hope; like a wick on a thick wax candle
That blocks the ear of mankind, it burns.
Perhaps this Covid era is our Dickensian nightmare;
Our Ebeneezer Scrooge moment;
Our chance to look to the inside and see what we possess that we may give.
Time to stop taking and expecting; time to be truly kind; time to really live.

The exasperation of Mrs Dickens

Well, Mr Charles Dickens, you're home at last!
You drift in here like the ghost of Christmas past
Expecting to see your supper on the table;
Well you can fend for yourself like that convict Abel
Magwitch you spend so much time with.

Don't give me one of your looks;
I'm not a character in one of those books
You present year after year
When your own family is sitting here,
Waiting to be taken notice of.

Oh, giving another one of your readings, were you?
And just what am I supposed to do?
You may think me soft, like the brothers Cheeryble
But *I'm not* soft and I'm not feeble,
Like that silly Dora Spenlow girl.

Night after night you're supping with Pickwick;
Your selfish grandiosity makes me sick!
No wonder you mix with that rotten Bill Sikes;
He shows a cruel streak that nobody likes
But still you keep churning them out.

And what of the fate of poor Little Nell?
That could be *your* child, who can tell
When you disregard them in favour of Heep.
I'm so tired of it, Charles, you make me weep
With frustration and despair.

Don't tell me it will all come good
As you tend the donkeys of Betsy Trotwood
And as for your friend, that lazy Skimpole,
Just what kind of a role
Model do you imagine him to be

To your children? Worried and neglected
In your absence; continually affected
By your dark moods and your need
For riches like that odious Smallweed.
Come, take off your coat.

I suppose I must be dogged like Inspector Bucket
But sometimes, Charles, I could just say... forget it!
I dream of going to France like Estella
Though I know you're not really such a bad fella
And I must make allowance for genius.

Just tell me I'm more important than Snodgrass;
Reassure me that you actually give an arse,
Then perhaps I could tolerate Scrooge and Cratchit.
Husband, let us make up and sit
Together, ever the best of friends.

St Francis School Days

1947, and he scoots along the street rolling a blue glass marble ahead,
Aimed at the red one just come to rest after being launched by his best mate.
He wins but at a cost as the last bus pulls away without him.
Another long walk home; another belt from his dad.

1967 and his daughter waits anxiously until she catches sight
Of her Mum and her Nan, standing behind all the other faces,
Her baby sister wrapped up in a second-hand Silver Cross pram.
They go to DiMarco's for an ice-cream.

1987 and his grandson kicks a ball around in the old playground.
He swops Top Trump cards with his friends
And eats peanut butter sandwiches for his lunch.
Later, he smiles as his Gramps tells him stories about the marbles
And how he put a book down his trousers
To take the sting out of the headmaster's slipper.

2020 and his little great granddaughter puts on her smart uniform
With the brown and yellow tie on elastic.
The sparkle in her eye matches his
As her news and chatter transport him back to that street,
The blue glass marble still rolling along.

The Saturday pictures Gang

Going to the pictures with my cousin;
If I sat too far back in the folding seat
I felt like I would disappear,
Swallowed up by a cinematic monster
In the half gloom.

The queue moved agonisingly slowly,
Swayed along by the chattering excitement.
At the booth, we paid our sixpence
Then we ran like a herd of frenzied cattle
To the warm womb

Of our childhood and the show would begin.
When the compère called for hush and the lights dimmed,
The projector began to purr
As the cartoon capers flickered into life.
We sat, bewitched.

A break was announced and we all filed down
The steps to buy an ice cream from the usher
Who had a tray hung from her neck,
Full of delights such as ice cream tubs and Fabs.
We were enriched

By the films; by the crowd; by our friendship.
We drew courage from our shared independence
At the Saturday picture show.
During the interval, birthdays were announced
And we all sang.

We clapped and cheered as the lights dimmed again
And Norman Wisdom's cheeky grin filled the screen
Or Laurel and Hardy appeared.
Our little hearts were fed on slapstick and fun.
We were the Saturday pictures gang.

Mouse's Revenge

'Hey, open that door,'
Said the mouse as he swore
To exact his revenge on the cat.

'He just ate my friend
And that isn't the end
Of the matter, just be sure of that!'

Mouse scampered away
For a year and a day
Then came back, all pumped up and mad.

He'd been at boot camp
Where he'd boxed as a champ;
He was mean, he was mighty and bad.

He spotted that cat
As it dozed on the mat
So he pounced and grabbed hold of its tail.

The cat gave a yelp
As he tried to get help
But his signals were all doomed to fail.

The man of the house,
It turned out, loved that mouse
That the cat had decided to eat.

He couldn't care less
For the moggie's distress
And was glad that, at last, he was beat.

40 and Judging

'When are you going to get your hair cut?'
'I'm sorry?'
'When are you going to get your hair cut?
You know, now that you're 40?'
'Oh, I don't know. Is it illegal, then?
To have long hair when you're 40?
Is it against the law?
What else should I know?
Must I keep my tits tucked in, for fear of
Offending the aged or the young
Because I'm not as pert as I once was?'
'Well, you look a bit odd... in jeans, I mean.'
'What?'
'Your thighs, they bulge a bit.'
'*And?* These are my thighs; they bulge a bit now.
What of it?'
'I'm just saying, that's all,
You're not as young as you were.'

'That's right, I'm 40
And if my long hair offends, if my bulging jeans embarrass,
If my sparkly make-up and dangly ear-rings cause giggles,
If my big bold bright jumper invites stares,
If my girly interest in pop music and film stars attracts sneers,
If my love of Drumsticks and Parma Violets and lolly pops hails sniggers,
If my determination to laugh and dance and sing
Makes them all watch in amazement or horror
Then good!
That means I'm not invisible
As you would have me be.'

Exclusivity

I want to live in a house that's exclusive
Like the one up the road on that nice new estate.
The kind that, to others, remains elusive
With its concrete driveway and wrought iron gate.
I want to wear those jeans the celebrities wear
With the stressed denim look and the knee holes cut out;
The sort that will have people stop and stare
As I strut around with my film star pout.
I want that offer on the new mobile phone;
The one made of gold; they've only got a few.
The one-off deal is aimed at me alone;
Exclusive, don't you know. It doesn't include you.
I want one of those cars with the four wheel drive
Where I can sit up high and look at those below.
The advert says it will make me feel alive
And take me anywhere I should desire to go.

I want to book the best holiday abroad
In a five star hotel with a nice guided tour
And if I find myself feeling somewhat bored
I could meet the locals who happen to be poor.
I'll live in my house on the gated estate,
Juliette balcony as a matter of course
And I'll let the environment meet its fate;
If no one else has one, I might install a horse.

Liar

What does it feel like when you are alone at night
And you think about the lies you've told?
Do you enjoy an indulgent satisfied smile?
Do you imagine with glee how bad you have made others feel
Or try and guess how much you have infected their lives?
Does your head buzz on a malignant high
After the cronies have scuttled back to where they came from,
Bored with your drama and your crocodile tears?
There you are, stripped of your audience;
Just you, alone in your own head.
Do you use that precious time to plan your next assault?
Is it all really that well thought out?
I don't think so.
How unhappy you must be to spoil the days of others
While your own life floats away
And your unnatural way of existing becomes normal for you.
Ultimately your lying keeps you down on the lowest rung of the ladder
And the rest of us climb over you,
Our tired heads held high.

Suffolk Breakers

For the thousandth time I pad across the cool grass,
My bare soles tickled and torn by the blades.
The sandy soil beneath soon settles soothingly between my toes
And again I am knocked backwards by a sight too Heavenly to describe;
All I can do is suck it up into my lungs.
The old timber breakers lay in peace
At the foot of the crumbling orange cliff.
In the morning, the North Sea will batter them from their slumber
As it did all those years ago when my children hid beneath them
With held breath, listening for the rush and squealing with cold and delight
When the waves smashed over the wood,
Down onto their little bodies and through their hair.
Tonight, the breakers snooze as the moonlight coruscates across the calm water
And the laser star beams bob around on the surface like silver fishes.
Yonder, the silhouette of Corton Church seems to grow broader
And the Suffolk ghosts whisper in my ear.
The groynes are submerged except for the pointed tips
Of ancient past-times wood slowly dying in a broth of salt and time.
They remind me of the transience of my existence
And reassure me that the tiny space I occupy on this Earth is not insignificant.

Us Girls

Remember when us girls went to the seaside?
We had not planned to drive that distance.
We meant only to have a look around the shops
Then you said, 'I don't fancy the shops on such a sunny day,'
So I said, 'I know, let's go to Hythe!'
And we did.
We talked all the way
Until we found ourselves parking up by the sea
And us two, like giggling schoolgirls,
Excitedly bought a mug of tea each and sat on the sea wall
To sip it with a sweet chocolate wafer.
We chatted and laughed and wondered
What our men would say when we told them.
I was so glad to be with you that day
Because the sadness hung about me
And if I had been alone looking at the sea,
I might have cried.

We took a walk along the High Street
Before having lunch in a nice cafe
Then we went back to the same spot by the sea
Where I had an ice cream and you had a strawberry lolly.
It was a wonderful day
And when we got home your man said,
'Was anyone fishing on the beach?'
And my man said,
'Cor, it was a great day for cycling along the seafront.'
We predicted they would say those things
And we were right.

A thought for Time

Each time I set out on the Present Road
I find myself on Thinking Lane
Then I'm dragged back by The Past
And squashed by The Future again

The man in the Suit

There sits the man in the suit,
Reading his book.
Neat haircut, clean shaven, his skin tanned
From all those golfing afternoons and short breaks away.

There sits the man in the jeans,
Checking his mobile phone.
Greasy hair pulled back into a pony tail, a goatee beard
And tattoos on his arms.

There sits the man in the suit,
His credit card tucked reassuringly inside his leather wallet
While the man in the jeans keeps a ten pound note
With some change in his pocket.

The man in the suit knows about stocks and shares
And managing his big pension.
The man in the jeans knows about love and hard work
And striving towards shared dreams.

The man in the jeans smiles at the people who pass by.
He notices the trees outside as he relaxes into his chair.
Then a woman with a small child enters the room,
Her belly swollen with baby.
In an instant, the man in the jeans insists she takes his seat
And he leans against the wall as they pass the time of day
together.

The man in the suit looks stiff and grim,
His hard face set as he keeps his eyes on the book that he
pretends to read.

Thief

Tell me, thief, who wears my brooch?
The one my son bought me when he went on a school trip to
Kew Gardens.
Or the ear-rings given to me by my second son?
The ones I pointed out in the shop with the blue shell inlay.
Is it your mother? Your sister? Your wife?
Or some unsuspecting punter at your local boot fair?

And the ear-rings my daughter gave me?
The silver ones with the little pink stones.
Where are they now?
What about the necklace my parents gave me years ago,
With the mother of pearl bird pendant?
Or my late grandmother's rosary beads?

Do you swing them around your head in triumphant glee?
Do you ever think of me?
Do you pass them around your friends as you share a beer?
Are you proud of yourself?
Does your work bring you cheer?

And the pearls my husband gave me
On our first wedding anniversary thirty nine years ago?
Or the necklace and ear-rings with the blue stone,
The matching ring of which is still on my right hand?

You would not have gained much money from your haul;
Invaluable in memories and emotions, that's all.

How many others have you hurt, thief?
Enjoy those short-lived highs you get
When you do what you do
For you live a miserable life
And your dirty deeds will always hang about you.

Buttercups

Brilliant yellow rays pierce my eyes and hit the back of my head;
They jump start my brain
And remind me that I am alive,
Side by side with the buttercups
And the daisies and the clover and the soft damp moss.
The buttercups capture my dark thoughts
In the centre of their souls
And throw them back at me, less dark; less heavy.
I feel faint as they all sing the same message, like a beauteous choir.
Their soft petals envelope me and wash away my gloom
With a message of faith and love.
I recover my balance and walk on
As I lock up those buttercups in my memory.
When I need them, I shall pull them out and
Their image will flow throughout my body,
Making my veins pulse with a happy rhythm;
Reminding me that I am alive.

Us two and you Two

Sitting up in our bed
On a springtime clad April morning,
Us two and you two.
You two, all concentration
As you suck on the teats and fill your bellies,
Your tiny fingers gripping the bottles
And your tiny toes wriggling around.
The room resonates with the sweet sound
Of your gentle slurps
And you look at us as we talk to you.
The room is full of love and contentment
As the dappled shadow of the trees outside
Dances on the wall at the end of our bed.

Then we wrap you up and take you out into the garden,
Us two holding you two.
We look at the speckled blossom on the pear tree
And touch the suede-like skin on the sumac.
We notice a bumble bee busy at work
And the bird song floats down upon us.
This day, framed now
And hanging in the corridor of our memories.
So special. So vital.
Us two and you two.

A new Morning

At first, I am not sure if it's moving;
I force my eyes to focus, concentrating hard
And yes, the grey cloud is moving away from me.
Way above it, the white stratocumulus cloudlets are spread out
Like half melted snow sliding off a roof.

Underneath all this, the deep, hot, orange orb of the sun
Begins to peep over the horizon.

The whole picture looks like the sea, lit by a soft glow lamp.
The grey clouds move on and disperse into the future,
Taking with them some of my black thoughts
And my world is draped in a new morning.

Snow

I watch it hit the window before sliding silently down into nothingness;
So I step outside into the cold.
The darkness of the night has been banished way above the world
And a warm magical glow enlivens us all.
A cocktail of exhilaration and fear quivers through my veins.
I take a few steps towards the damson tree;
The snow sits heavy on the skinny branches
Before falling with a soft thud onto the blanket below.
I notice the frosted glass footsteps of the young fox
And I wonder where he is now in this other world of cotton wool clouds
And tissue paper tears that stick to my eyelashes.
In the morning, perhaps it will be deeper and softer and more brilliant
And I will awake to the sound of no traffic on the road.
Or perhaps, as I sleep, it will rain
And I'll wake up to the drip, drip as it all melts and turns to slush,
Running along gutters and falling into drains
And the world will feel dull and damp and gloomy.

Either way, this night is one to remember;
This night has been blessed with a gift from Mother Nature.
This night I could smell the snow;
My tired body enjoyed the silence;
I breathed it all in,
Then stored it away in my mind's pantry
For those days in the future
When my spirit needs feeding.

Father Christmas has a bad Day

I met Father Christmas the other day.
'Can't chat,' he said, 'I must be on my way.
I've presents to wrap and labels to write;
I'm sure, at this rate, I'll be up all night.
I need to shine up my black wellie boots
And dust off one of my red and white suits.
I need to sort out the elves' Christmas do;
You know, they can be a troublesome crew.
They say the shift work is bad for their health
And declare they want a cut of my wealth.'
'What wealth?' I asked. 'Well, *exactly*,' he said,
'And the responsibility's all on my head.
I'm thinking of packing the whole lot in;
No matter what I do, I just can't win.'
'Well, Father Christmas,' said I with a smile,
'Why don't you sit down and rest for a while?
Let me buy you a nice cup of strong tea
And a piece of cake. I'm sure then you'll see
That sometimes things just get on top of us
And we forget that life can be fabulous.'

As we sat in the caf, I ventured to say,
'I'm sure Mrs Christmas helps in her way?'
'No,' he growled, 'she's gone off to find herself,
Left a steak pie and a note on the shelf.'
'Perhaps,' I offered, 'that may do you good,
Absence makes the heart... you know... and you could
Get on with your rounds while she has a break.'
He nodded assent as he ate his cream cake.
We drained out the pot and watched the snow fall.
'I might keep this job,' he smiled, 'after all,
Who else gets to light up the world's children's eyes
As they open their gifts and I get my mince pies?

People would miss Rudolph and the team;
They're part of the wonderful Christmas dream.
I stock pile the carrots – they last us all year
And then there's the sherry….and the odd beer.
It's all about kindness and love and thought
And never about the things that are bought.
So thank you for that, I'm very much cheered,'
And his smile shone through his marvellous beard.
I stood in the snow as he walked away;
Poor Father Christmas – he just had a bad day.

JCC

I want to be like you, John Cooper Clarke;
I just want to park
Myself on the great poetic stage.
I want people to take note of what I do,
Like they do for you;
I want people to listen to me.
I want to be seen; I want to stand out.

I'm all about madness and people and love.
Why can't others see, I've got things to say
In my own unique way?

I'm not you, John Cooper Clarke, for sure.
I could emulate you, I know I could
And perhaps I should
Because that way, I might be noticed.

I don't possess your insight or your wit
But I'm not... bad;
I could at least aim to be like you.

It's difficult for me to be scary
And I'm not sweary.
I just own those traits that make me *me*.
So remember my name, John Cooper Clarke.
I *will* make my mark,
You'll see. Then you'll wish you were like me.

Being 50

It isn't like being twenty one, being fifty;
We're not nifty or fit as a flea;
We suffer if we stay up too late
And we're just a little slower than we used to be.
And thirty feels a long way back, when we are fifty;
At thirty they say we reach our peak.
At fifty, we're on the way back down
And life's rucksack on our backs can make our legs feel weak.

Being forty feels like yesterday, when we're fifty.
We may carry a little more meat
And have trouble with indigestion;
We use muscle rub and special insoles for our feet.
On the other hand, at fifty, we know where we are;
None of the angst of those younger years.
We can walk with an assured swagger
As we cast off pointless energy-consuming fears.

Though, annoyingly, at fifty, we're not quite sixty.
We don't get the free swimming lessons
And, although we may look the right age,
We're not entitled to older people's concessions.
Assistants aren't quite sure as they look us up and down
Before asking, 'special rates today?'
We smile sweetly and enquire of them,
'Do I look sixty, dear?' and they don't know what to say.

At fifty, we like to know there's a toilet nearby;
We're proud if we can stand on one leg.
Some of our teeth are real and some are not
And we like to make sure we eat our daily boiled egg.
We read magazine articles about supplements;
We buy lycra and start to work out
When we're fifty. Then we tell ourselves
We've still got it; and decide to shake it all about.

At fifty, we're not considered young and we're not old;
I'd call myself an in-betweeny.
Fancy meeting at the beach for some fun?
If you wear your budgie smugglers, I'll wear my bikini.

On a steam train on the Watercress Line

If I walk quickly enough
And I go far enough
Do you think I could turn back the clock?
Do you think I could catch life from behind
And demand that it stop making me its mock?

If I walk slowly enough
And I fall back enough
Do you think I might be left alone?
Do you think I could summon up the strength
To lift and cast off this stone around my neck?

If I shout loudly enough
And I jump high enough
Do you think anyone would spot me?
Do you think I would be noticed out there
And humanity could see that I matter?

If I speak softly enough
And I tip toe enough
Do you think the world would fall asleep?
Do you think that a calm might envelope me
As those things that make me weep fade to nothing?

But then,
If I smile enough
And if I'm kind enough
Do you think everyone would join in?
Do you think we could respect each other
And dare to hope we can begin to learn something?

Social Denial

Do they ever look at *real* photographs?
Handle them, smell them, treasure them?
Do they ever unplug themselves
And slip into the concrete world?
In our age of wifi and make believe
And faceless relations,
Some of us are ignored, condemned or dismissed,
Killed by the search engine.
Some of us have lives that are not media perfect;
But it's *real* life and, surely, better to embrace than to deny?
We just *like* each other and try to be kind.
We talk to each other at the bus stop and in the doctor's surgery.
We don't live on the edge, waiting for the ping or the shudder of the next message;
The next vital communication that drags us further out of reach.
We don't have all the answers
But maybe if they step out of their browsers
And join us in the real world,
Together, we could become a force for good.

Tiny Steps

With tiny steps, I creep towards old age,
Happily oblivious to all it may bring
Until the day I experience a revelation;
That one day you may be gone.
Then how shall I live, without the one
Who makes my heart sing or makes me feel mad?
You're just there, even when I'd like you not to be;
And you're there, when I really need you to be.
What happens to me if I find you're no longer in your place?

I absolutely know that, no matter how tiny my steps,
One day, my day could come
And I shall be exposed,
No longer tucked underneath your wing,
No longer hidden in your shadow.

Rain on Me

Come then, rain on me:
Love, guilt, angst, joy, fear and all.
I have my rain mac.

Feel

Someone once told me
That you're as young as you feel.
What if you don't feel?

Umbrella

Poor fly that crawled into the folds of my umbrella
Only to die;
It dropped to the floor as I prepared to open the door
And step out into the rain.
Poor you who opened your umbrella inside
And your mother told you that's why your granny died;
It must have caused you pain.
Poor bloke who gripped his brolly in the wind
And found himself pinned to the railings
Outside Rochester Cathedral
Where he found time to contemplate his failings.
Poor me; no umbrella big enough
To shield me from the world
And all that stuff.

The pain splits me in Two

The pain creeps up on me and it splits me in two
Like a log torn asunder by one blow from an axe.
I fall one way to despair and the other to oblivion

But in my head I'm walking, walking and walking,
Somewhere towards where there is no more thinking;
Somewhere my exhausted self can sleep.

Then, like in a science fiction movie,
Each of my two parts begins to slither along the ground and slide upwards
Until I realise I am still standing.

As I look around, nobody has noticed this catastrophic happening
So I sit down at a table and order a coffee.
I think I'm in a silent movie; the waitress hears my words but I don't.

It's lurking there; the pain.
It's in my bag or on my back or in that mirror on the wall.
I can smell it as still it creeps up on me
And always, it splits me in two.

Child of Change

I dreamt of you last night
As my troubled brain jumped and skipped
Around in my hot skull.
You rolled in with an angry roar,
Your own troubles torturing you
And you begged for my help.
I stupidly mumbled some glib remark
About climate change and human error
So you sucked yourself out
And rolled back in with a terrifying screech.
I fell to my knees and cried out
In my impotent desperate state
For I didn't know how to pacify you.
Then I became aware of them;
Tiny dots running across the shingle;
Tiny wings flying above your angry white foam.

They grew bigger and I realized that each one was a child of
this world;
Each little face smiling with grim determination.
'Things will change, 'they chanted, 'things will change,'
And their voices grew so loud I feared my head would explode.
I heard you chuckle as you drew them around you
For some assignation to which I was not invited.
Then thousands of children skipped past me, towards the hills
And more flew gently away towards the horizon.
'I'm sorry I couldn't help,' I whimpered
With a shrug of my shoulders.

You smiled at me and rolled out with a satisfied sigh.

The Rooks

Who can tell the intentions of the rooks
As they stand and stare, their beady eyes tunnel-like
In their frightening depth?
What symbolic feathers on their backs
Where man's breath smoothes them to a gloss.
What can they tell me about this place?
Why are they here in this dangerous, terrifying gloom?
My imagination catapults me into their world
And I am trapped.
Maybe the end is waiting for me;
It's my welcome to this world-forgotten place.
The rooks cackle and laugh at my discomfort.
Their claws wrap themselves around my bravery
And squeeze it out of me until I am on my knees.
I close my eyes and pray;
Pray as the rooks in their religious finery sneer at me
And tell me how bad I am.
This is the end and they expect me to beg forgiveness.

Bob Ross

Hey, Bob Ross, I didn't know you back then
But I'm so glad I found you now.
You are the justification for television repeats;
You are my encouragement to pick up a brush;
You are my confidence in myself
And my belief that I can do something.
You are my source of good feeling;
You are my happy little cloud and my almighty tree;
You are my fantastic sky.
You make me feel free for half an hour every day.
Thank you, Bob Ross, and God bless.

Yesterdays

Last night, I visited my yesterdays.
I was unprepared for the feelings
That muddied the waters of life
Back then, as they sidled up
And leapt on my back.
Thoughts stormed through my head
As I stumbled,
Pit against
My foe:
Time.
I fell
Through a door
That led me back
To the here and now
Where I sat on the floor.
I needed to make a choice;
To stay back? Or to stride on ahead?
Claw by claw, I prized off the demons
And marched into the unknown, with a smile.

Come love me, Autumn

How I have missed you, my love.
You left me last year, painfully slowly; so cruel, so cruel.
Left me to the harsh cold of Winter;
The bitter wind made me cry like a child,
My bright pink fingers throbbing with pain.
But come, I am not angry.
You are here now, come back to find me
So wrap your arms around my shoulders while I tell you how I rallied
When Spring called me through the fog.
She wiped away my tears and made me smile.
Spring injected me with life and made my head buzz.
The slow motion flower heads and rich scents sucked up my depression.
The hum and click, the trill and whisper led me dancing to the edge of Summer.
Look, my skin bears the sun's hot kiss and happy freckles map my face.
I love you, dear Autumn;
You bring me calm and security that nothing else can give.
Hold me, please. Breathe softly over me
As I allow myself to sleep a while.
Let us not think about you going but enjoy this magical time
As we colour and glow together.

Christmas Years

She was just four years of age
When Father Christmas sat in the front room
And watched as she tore off the wrapping paper
To reveal a toy grand piano; it was pink and white.

Then the years fluttered by as she held on to their wings;
The frost still burns her throat and the sweet robin still sings.

The mobile shop stopped outside
And she ran to fetch her pocket money
Before looking at the cheap gifts on display.
She chose a red velvety reindeer especially for her Nan.

Then the years fluttered by as she held on to their wings;
The frost still burns her throat and the sweet robin still sings.

Shyly, she lifted the box;
It was roughly wrapped and tied with ribbon.
She still has that ribbon tucked away somewhere
With the name tag covered in kisses. She still wears that scent.

Then the years fluttered by as she held on to their wings;
The frost still burns her throat and the sweet robin still sings.

She sat down for a breather
After getting their children into bed
And, while they softly dreamed of Christmas magic,
She placed the presents under the tree while he poured a drink.

Then the years fluttered by as she held on to their wings;
The frost still burns her throat and the sweet robin still sings.

She sat down for a breather
As her children's children begged her to play.
'Just one more game, just one more go,' they pleaded
So she jumped into her memories and joined in the fun.

Then the years fluttered by as she held on to their wings;
The frost still burns her throat and the sweet robin still sings.

She gently held her roses
As she trudged slowly through the thin crisp snow.
From her bag, she took out a cloth and polished
Before placing the blooms in water. She stood back, smiling.

Then the years fluttered by as she held on to their wings;
The frost still burns her throat and the sweet robin still sings.

Then the years fluttered by as she held on to their wings;
And the sweet robin still sings.

Early morning home Town

I set out in the early morning mist, walking the back roads and
Heading for The Vines. Once a vineyard then pasture land for cattle,
At this time of the day it provides a little world of peace and quiet.
As I stroll along the short avenue of plane trees, I meet a man sitting on a bench.
I smile a cheery 'good morning' and he nods at me as he feeds the pigeons.
The cathedral, the second oldest in England, looks frighteningly magnificent
As the sunlight clothes the ethereal spire in a pink haze.
In the tiny burial ground, I see a squirrel running along the low wall;
Nonchalant pigeons strut around on the ground looking for breakfast
And a couple of robins are squabbling over one little perch in the yew tree.
My ear is drawn to the drone of a bumblebee as it lands on a child's headstone.
There are a few: 1843, 6 months; 1844, 6yrs 8 months, 1853, 17 months;
Testimony to those poor Victorian families who once walked these pavements.
The bumblebee works on, inspecting the roses as the bells toll and the choir sings.
A dog walker crosses the road; a lone ambler like me smiles as he walks on.
A couple of breathless runners skim past me and a family chatters by,
Probably heading for the play park down by the river.
In the lazy Sunday High Street, shopkeepers and café owners are setting up
And above all this life, as the haze lifts and the sun shines brightly,
Rochester Castle is revealed in all its awesome splendour,
Reminding me of my place in history.

Notes to Poems

When Robert Burns came to Tea

My first anthology was entitled 'A Walk with Charles Dickens and Other Poems.' For this, my second collection, I wanted to continue the theme and imagine doing something ordinary yet extraordinary with another famous writer. I chose Robert Burns, fondly regarded as the national poet of Scotland. He died in 1796 aged just 37 years and ever since, Burns Night is held in January to celebrate his life and works. In 2018, I was invited to the medieval market town of Faversham to perform on Burns Night and this is the poem I especially wrote for the occasion.

I was privileged to be included in the same line up that night as the late poet and artist Rosemary McLeish who was originally from Glasgow. I know Rosie liked my poem because she kindly told me so. She was a woman of awesome talent who inspired me then and still does now.

The ladder in my Tights

If you have read my work before, you will know that I like to play around with rhyme and structure in my poetry. This one is a bit of fun that started around the expression 'A over T' which I first heard uttered by a headteacher I worked for when I was supply teaching. It was winter and the lady said we needed to get the ground salted as 'we don't want anyone going A over T.' It took me a while to realise what she meant and so grew the ladder in my tights. We all know what it feels like when things go wrong sometimes.

We're on the same Road

We are all walking the same road, aren't we? Perhaps some of us should have a little more patience and show a little more kindness towards those people who don't find the road so easy and those who need to take things a little slower. Don't be in a hurry to overtake but stop and say hello sometimes.

The river from Rochester Pier

I have lived in Rochester for 17 years; there is much history here and in the Medway towns in general. My favourite story teller, Charles Dickens, loved this area and took much inspiration from it. The prison hulks featured in his work Great Expectations would have been moored around this area and The Guildhall Museum in Rochester High Street has a wonderful exhibition depicting the hard life of prisoners on board the decommissioned ships.

From the pier one can hop on a boat and sail out into the Medway Estuary and beyond. I did so and saw close up the Red Sand Towers or forts, seven anti-aircraft towers used in the second world war, abandoned now yet still eerily imposing.

Water is important to me; calming and life affirming. The River Medway is a tidal river and so, to me, very close to being by the sea. Watching from the pier or sitting on a bench high up in the castle grounds, my mind can sail away for hours at a time and I am grateful to have such a wonder on my door step.

**Since writing this, Rochester Pier has been closed for essential repairs and part of the floating pontoon has collapsed into the water; efforts are being made to raise funds to make this area accessible to the public again.

In the woods with Mum and Dad

This poem recalls a walk with my parents in the local woods near their home. We were determined to make our way to a bench in the middle of the growth and it was worth it, to sit together catching the sunshine on our faces while we listened to the wind whispering through the trees along with the birdsong.

As we picked our way back along the uneven pathways, we weren't prepared for the mud and the bracken in the darker more shaded areas. My childhood anxieties did not appear but different worries arose and I held on tight to Mum's hand as Dad led the way holding her other. I know they felt it too and I breathed an inward sigh of relief when we emerged out into the open. We had survived our daring adventure.

When we were Young

Life changes. Love changes.

The ghost of a life lived: Violet

Some way from the Medway Bridge Marina, there is a little cluster of river dwellings. On a walk one day, I came across this particular disused yard and boathouse; the discovery was eerie but wonderful. It was clear that someone had once lived here and, fastened to a wire panel at the front of the property, was a tatty old post box with the name 'Violet' painted on it. It looked a bit sad so I decided to write this poem as a tribute to the mysterious Violet.

Higher and Wider

This poem recalls and celebrates the madness, the fun, the ups and the downs of young family life in our little end of terrace in the village of Eccles in Aylesford.

Higher and Wider II

It all trickled through our fingers and then it was gone. 'They grow up too soon;' 'life's so short;' 'time goes so fast' and so on. How many more clichés can you bring to mind? The thing is, oft repeated clichés are exactly that because their messages are true and passed down the generations. Take heed and enjoy.

The tears won't Stop

We all interact with people, on one level or another and we have no idea what is going on in their lives or what may have gone before and troubles them still. I have become adept at managing the grief I feel at the loss of my granddaughter and I am always aware that the dam could burst at any time. It's tiring but it's made me a kinder, more tolerant person.

The world and Beyond

Do you remember when you were five, like Penny? I cling on to the child within this aged body and time spent with my grandchildren allows me to stop being a grown up for a while. We all need to escape sometimes so remember to feed the fun side.

Wonderwall

Grace reminds me how important it is to dance in the kitchen now and again.

The drunk and the Druggie

I was inspired to write this poem by yet another 'celebrity scoop' doing the rounds. In a world where we have more materials and possessions than ever before, there seems to be a growing discontent and frustration. Could our unhappy malady be something to do with us forgetting our debt towards all powerful Nature and that, to embrace and protect our natural world is the only way to properly feel alive?

The candle in the Library

I am privileged to be involved with the independent literary arts organisation Wordsmithery which is based in Medway. Through Wordsmithery, I have grown as a writer, being challenged and encouraged to take part in open mic sessions, literary festivals and writing workshops. I have also been commissioned to contribute work to various projects.

This poem was composed during a workshop at Gillingham Library and the idea was to put my hand in a bag and draw out an object, about which I would write. 'My cloak' refers to my cloak of grief which I wear every day. You can find the poem in my first anthology. That was a great day, meeting people, sharing ideas with writers and feeling included.

Old People

I wrote this blank verse poem after visiting a public house in Lympne, near Hythe in Kent. I was enjoying a nice pub lunch when my attention was caught by an old couple as they crossed the road. Watching their world from the sidelines was incredibly moving.

Inferior

This is a bit of fun and it always goes down well when I perform it to an audience. I think most of us have experienced a time when we felt inferior or out of place and this can excite different emotions in different people.

Five pairs of eyes looking at my Thing

Bit personal but I've had several visits to the gynaecological department at Medway Hospital over the years. Great staff who do a wonderful job but they'll never take away the embarrassment so I thought the best thing to do was to get it out in the form of a poem. The Bee Gees, of course, are the best ever and always will be.

On my own in the Cafe

I like to sit on my own in a cafe and often read or write whilst there. One of the recurring themes in my work is the exploration of feelings and how well we hide them at times. This poem is constructed using a simple rhyming pattern within each three line stanza. Perhaps the simplicity belies the subject matter just as our smiling faces sometimes hide what's inside our hearts.

Moon II

The poem 'Moon' is included in my first anthology. Moon II is a continuing celebration of the moon which has always fascinated me and fed my soul.

Niamh's Song

This poem celebrates the life of my little granddaughter who died of sepsis in 2015. In my family, she is and always will be a big part of our lives and I know that one day we will meet her again.

Why would I Imagine?

It is too hard, trying to imagine what might have been and better to accept what happened is done and cannot be changed. There will always be reminders though; whispers and imaginings, milestones and anniversaries. Accepting isn't easy.

Boxley Beginnings

Boxley Village, just outside Maidstone, is as unspoiled today as it was all those years ago when my husband and I lived seven years there with our three small children. We had very little, buying our household possessions at the auction in Maidstone market place by the river Medway. In Boxley, with my little family, I spent some of the happiest days of my life.

New Year's Day with You

I live with a gentle constant sadness and I know my husband feels it too. The beginning of another year brings it to the fore and my favourite place of refuge and repair is beside the sea at Hythe. So this is where we go, often.

There are no Fairies

Nothing matches the imagination of a child and I relish the chances I get to enter the worlds my grandchildren inhabit. This poem was inspired when I realised my grandson, Thomas, no longer believed there were fairies living in the long grass by the sumac trees in our garden. The dinosaurs are still out there though.

In the sea at Hythe

No matter how often I look out at the sea, listen to it or wade in and give myself up to the waves, the thrill I feel, along with the awe, can sometimes be overwhelming. What stories, what histories, what might, what majesty, what steady comfort in an unsettled world. In this poem, I included internal rhyme; the third and fourth lines in each stanza.

Beard Logic

You work it out.

A Dickens 2020

I was commissioned to write some Charles Dickens themed poems to perform at the Dickens Festival in Rochester. Dickens lived from 1812 until 1870. This work compares times back then with times now and includes references to some of the wonderful characters he created. As I wrote, we were all living through the Covid era which made me think about some aspects of modern life and how, surely, two of the most important human behaviours must be simple kindness and gratitude.

The exasperation of Mrs Dickens

This is a bit of fun. It is well documented that Dickens was not the best of husbands and perhaps did not pay his wife the kindness and respect she deserved. So I decided to let Catherine Dickens let rip and put her husband in his place, with reference to some of my favourite characters in my favourite Dickens novels.

St Francis school Days

St Francis Roman Catholic School was situated at the top of Week Street in Maidstone. The building is still there but the school has moved to more modern premises out of town. My father went there with his siblings, I went there with my cousins, my children attended and now two of my grandchildren love it. Family history rolling along like that blue glass marble.

The Saturday pictures Gang

My cousin, Kim and I grew up together, spending many happy days in the countryside when our parents worked on farms. This poem recalls the fun and the innocence of those times when we went to the Saturday pictures in Maidstone. My favourites were Norman Wisdom, Laurel and Hardy, Abbott and Costello and cartoons like Tom and Jerry. I remember going to the pictures with my Mum to see The Wizard of Oz and Dickens' A Christmas Carol with Albert Finney. I linked each pair of stanzas with the last word on the last line.

Mouse's Revenge

Just a bit of fun and playing around with rhyme.

40 and Judging

This poem was inspired by the memory of someone telling me that, as I had turned 40, I should get my hair cut. I'm twenty years older than that now; I still have long hair and I'm more comfortable than I've ever been just being me. It isn't easy in this digital media obsessed society but I'm happy to let it all ride on by. So pass the Parma Violets and put on a bit of Madness or the Bee Gees before time runs out.

Exclusivity

Have you noticed how everything seems to be exclusive these days? Exclusive offers in the shops, exclusive offers online, exclusive housing developments, exclusive introductory offers pushed uninvited through our letter boxes? It's all very silly and meaningless so I wrote a poem to make fun of the idea. Anyway, as human beings, is it not kinder and nobler and more comfortable to be inclusive?

Liar

If you have ever been the target of a liar, you will know why I had to write this poem. They know they are liars and I don't believe there can be many people who would be happy to know that of themselves.

Suffolk Breakers

Each year, we took our children to a caravan site in the village of Corton, between Lowestoft and Great Yarmouth. We had little money and sometimes had to go in off-peak season when the weather could be a bit wild. If we went in the summer, we were bronzed by the wind and the sunshine. A set of wooden steps led us down to the beach where we frolicked in the North Sea. I went back once and found the steps collapsed as the cliffs eroded around them. I don't think I'll go back again.

Us Girls

I wrote this after a day out with my friend, Janet. We reminded ourselves of the fun and the delight in sometimes doing things spontaneously. I don't know if she knew how much her company meant to me that day; her chatter and her laughter and her listening ear. We had a great time, us girls.

A thought for Time

This simple poem sums up my struggle with living in the now. I try to keep the past from overshadowing the here and now and to leave the future to itself. It is hard work and sometimes impossible but I keep trying.

The man in the Suit

I wrote this poem after observing two very different looking men in a waiting room. I built their characters around their appearance which of course, I wouldn't do in real life. Then I weaved my story around them. That's the great thing about poetry; I can draw inspiration from real life or I can choose to let my imagination run free, amassing a mind catalogue of my very own people, places and events.

Thief

Some years ago, my home was burgled. The culprit took all of my jewellery including my late grandmother's rosary beads, passed on to me by my mother. None of my jewellery was worth much money; all of it was worth the world in sentimental value. Like every other first time victim, this event was something I had only ever heard about and not one I would have dreamed ever happening to me. It affected me very much and, unhappy Christian that I am, I hope something bad happens to that thief and all likeminded criminals.

Buttercups

I think you know now that the miracle of Nature, the wonder and the beauty of all it provides and offers, are things that nurture and sustain me as I travel through my life. Nature lifts me, reminding me that the nonsense and the horror of this world are both human driven and transient. Nature is the only constant so I hold on with confidence. And buttercups are beautiful, aren't they?

Us two and you Two

This poem recalls the most wonderful time spent with my husband and our grandchildren, twins Niamh and Thomas. Their Mummy and Daddy had gone out for the evening so the babies stayed overnight with us. They were just ten months old. The love; the joy; I am transported back just typing this note. I am grateful that we had that time without being aware of the black cloud approaching us. Niamh died and went to Heaven just two weeks later.

A new Morning

I probably think too much and I am easily affected by the swirl of life that surrounds me. And, if I am honest with myself, life is harder since my eldest granddaughter died. I look to Nature more and more to keep me going. This poem was inspired by the view from my bedroom window. I like to look beyond the roof tops each morning and take in the sky.

Snow

This poem is another celebration of Nature and depicts the wonder of snow, especially in the evening light. I particularly like the last four lines as they sum up my relationship with Nature. I have noticed that, when I am most affected or when I want to express my darker thoughts, I am more likely to write in blank verse rather than rhyme.

Father Christmas has a bad Day

This poem is a bit of fun and yes, of course Father Christmas is real!

JCC

John Cooper Clarke, a punk poet in the 70s, is a brilliant performance poet to whom I aspire. He is a thoughtful and intelligent man, a brilliant writer and I will never equal him but it's fun aiming for something on the fringes of his talent.

Being 50

Well, what can I say? It isn't always easy, this getting older lark, but I'm grateful to be given a shot at it. The most important things for me are to try not to take life too seriously, to be kind, to have fun and to remember my place on this Earth.

On a steam train on the Watercress Line

I have enjoyed a few coach trips, some on my own and some with my friend, Debbie. This one was interesting as I travelled solo and very few people in the party wanted to interact with me. It seemed that my aloneness made them uncomfortable though I was clearly ok with it and enjoying myself. The experience got me thinking about how odd we humans can be. This poem took shape as I sat on a lovely old steam train after a visit to Jane Austen's house in Chawton, Hampshire.

Social Denial

I worry about today's obsession with social media and all things online. As human beings, we are made to interact socially face to face, to make and do, to problem solve, to fetch and carry, to be active and involved with each other. Our children are becoming addicted to screens, addicted to social media, overweight and depressed because they don't mix and move. Society is losing something vital and we're slipping into a virtual world of horror. We need to start talking again.

Tiny Steps

This poem deals with the idea of a couple being parted by death after a long time together. It is both terrifying and awfully fascinating and whenever the unwelcome thought creeps into my mind I chase it out as quickly as I am able.

Rain on Me

Life; bring it on.

Feel

The haiku, with its syllabic pattern of 5, 7, 5, allows one to pack a lot into a small space. I like a haiku.

Umbrella

I wrote this poem during a workshop run by Wordsmithery in Rochester Library. My Mum has always told me that it's bad luck to put up an umbrella indoors. And don't put new shoes on the table.

The pain splits me in Two

Many times, I have dragged myself out through the front door however unhappy or tired I may be. Most of us know how that feels but we do it anyway. We keep going, carrying our stuff around with us.

Child of Change

This poem is inspired by my worry about climate change and my feeling of powerlessness in the face of world crisis. The driving character in this piece is the all powerful sea and I believe our salvation can only be delivered by re-connecting with Nature; we need to remember and accept that we do not own this Earth we live on. We are custodians; guardians of something that governs the survival of us and all species. We must learn to behave responsibly and be less greedy. I feel that, armed with awareness, knowledge and compassion, our younger generations especially have the power to change things for the better.

The Rooks

This poem was inspired by the rooks I saw outside Rochester Cathedral. Charles Dickens' last unfinished novel, The Mystery of Edwin Drood, was set around the town and in the cathedral itself. It is a tale of disappearance and possible murder, ideas mingled here with my fear of dark spaces and the unknown.

Bob Ross

Bob Ross was a talented artist and tutor who presented a television series, The Joy of Painting which aired in the US, UK and other countries. I did not see these programmes first time around but watched them when they were aired again in this country during the Covid crisis. What a kind, intelligent, thoughtful and inspirational man who encouraged everyone to have a go. Nature was his greatest influence and his paintings were beautiful. I did not miss an episode of his show and this poem is my thank you.

Yesterdays

I enjoyed experimenting with structure here, producing a concrete poem; an egg timer full of time. It is a lesson to myself to keep looking forward rather than back; that learning and changing are so much more powerful than fretting and regretting.

Come love me, Autumn

I like to personify aspects of Nature and autumn is a favourite season of mine. Still drowsy from the summer sunshine, I love to watch the subtle changes taking place. If you look closely, Nature gives us something wonderful to see every day of the year. The signs of new life and the growth never stop.

Christmas Years

Some aspects of this poem are lifted from my own life as I imagine one woman's lifetime. I had that little piano, left by my Dad dressed up as Father Christmas. I bought that velvety reindeer for my Nan from the mobile shop in the big green van that stopped outside our rural home in East Peckham. At 60 years, I sometimes think about how my life has played out and wonder how it may end.

Early morning home Town

It's nice sometimes to write a poem in blank verse; to simply put down what I see or what I feel, without spending my time and energy agonising over precise words or working on the rhyming pattern, both of which I do a lot and happily so. Sometimes it feels good to let the words and ideas flow in the now, capturing life in its immediacy. Early morning is the best time of the day for me and I never tire of meandering around the streets of Rochester; it relaxes me and makes me feel good to be alive.

About the Author

I was born and brought up in the Kentish countryside. I had stories included in two well-known popular magazines before my first anthology A Walk with Charles Dickens and Other Poems was published in 2018. My work has been commissioned, most recently for the Dickens Festival in my home town of Rochester and for a collection put together to raise money for The Bumblebee Conservation Trust. As well as composing and performing poetry, I give talks on the joy and the process of writing.

A very special person once told me that Nature just is; makes no excuses, needs no reasons. The natural world looks after my well-being; it feeds my imagination and makes me feel a part of something wonderful and mysterious. Together with Love, people and everyday life, Nature provides me with never-ending inspiration for my writing.

Among my literary influences are Dickens, Austen, Shakespeare, Wordsworth, Hardy, Pam Ayres, Paulo Coelho, especially The Alchemist and Eckhart Tolle whose book The Power of Now is my go-to book when my peace of mind needs restoring. Sarah Winman's A Year of Marvellous Ways was given to me as a gift; set in Cornwall, it is haunting and beautiful and it touched my soul. Laura Lynne Jackson confirms for me what I already know; that is, life on this Earth is only part of the journey and Wm Paul Young confirms this for me in his wonderful book The Shack which made me cry. Gyles Brandreth is a fantastic man of words and his book Dancing by the Light of the Moon promotes the enjoyment and the benefits to be had from reading and learning poetry. I gave a copy of this book to each of my children and my husband and I read it together. These writers are just a few who inspire me and affect me; there are too many more to list here.

This collection, as the last, includes poems that celebrate the life of my little granddaughter Niamh who died in 2015 at the age of ten and a half months. Like many families, we were robbed of someone beautiful by the curse of sepsis. My husband Frank and I continue to enjoy the company and delights of Niamh's twin brother, our grandson, and our three younger granddaughters. There are no adequate words to express the joy they bring into our lives.

I continue to write poetry and I'm exploring story writing a bit more now. I wrote and performed 'Cerebral City' for a project run by Wordsmithery during the Covid lockdown. You can find out more at www.hereticsassemble.com I was commissioned to write and perform for the Welcome to Cloisterham day 2021 and 2022, both held in Rochester around the castle. I have also been invited along to local WI groups to give readings and talk about the art and enjoyment of poetry.

I still work as an administrator for my local library, registration and archive service. I also work one morning a week as a volunteer administrator for the Kent based charity Demelza Hospice Care for Children. These two roles bring me a sense of purpose; in a small way, I make a difference in the world.

Thank you for taking the time to explore this anthology of mine. I hope you find reason to laugh and reason to think. Perhaps these poems will inspire you to seek out more poets or maybe have a go at writing a few lines yourself.

Life has its ups and its downs but I keep walking onwards. I hope you do too.

Bridget Nolan 2022

Acknowledgements

Thank you, Mum and Dad, for the chats and the laughs over iced coffee and cake. Together, we live in the here and now.

My thanks to James Essinger of The Conrad Press for his time and his kindness and for his invaluable advice. Thank you also to Charlotte Mouncey for the typesetting and the great cover design; you somehow made my imagination real. I am very grateful to you both for helping me bring this anthology to fruition.

Lastly, and especially, thank you to Sam and Barry of Wordsmithery. You do so much for the promotion of all things literary in Medway. Through your encouragement and belief in my ability, I have grown as a writer and a performer of words. And for everyone at The UK Sepsis Trust www.sepsistrust.org